Duality of Existance

ARJUNARAO KAZA

Clever Fox® PUBLISHING
Chennai • Bangalore

CLEVER FOX PUBLISHING
Chennai, India

Published by CLEVER FOX PUBLISHING 2026

ISBN: 978-93-7500-503-2

ACKNOWLEDGEMENT

I am deeply grateful to ChatGpt in refining and structuring the manuscript of Duality of existence.

CONTENTS

CHAPTER 1

BEFORE CREATION – THE SILENT GROUND**

Human language and concepts are inadequate to fully describe the state before creation because the human concepts are formed within time and space and created reality. Any description of the pre-creation state can only be approximate and symbolic and not exact and complete.

There existed two divine primordial entities surrounded by void of infinite dimensions, which had neither beginning nor ending before creation. These entities are of infinite mass and density. There was complete stillness, and there existed neither time nor space.

Human language and concepts are inadequate to fully describe the state of existence before creation. Human language is descriptive and experiential whereas science is mathematical and operational. Both are formed within time and space and therefore describe relationships that came into existence. Hence procreation state where time and space do not exist cannot be envisaged.

The silent environment that was present was not passive in an ordinary sense. It contained potential but not intention. It held a possibility but not a direction. In this stillness, there was no conflict, no distinction, no moment and therefore no creation. Creation requires difference; silence is complete because it lacks division.

The human tendency is to imagine creation as an act — a sudden event, a decision, a will. But creation is better understood as a transition rather than an action: a movement from unity to multiplicity, from stillness to expression. The silent void did not choose to create; creation emerged when balance gave way to polarity.

Scientific analogies can only gesture toward this idea. Science cannot describe what lies beyond measurement; it can only acknowledge the boundary. That boundary is where philosophy and spirituality begin — not in opposition to science, but in continuity with it.

The silent void was timeless, yet time would arise from it. It was spaceless, yet space would unfold within it. It was formless, yet all forms would eventually appear from its depths. Nothing was missing in that state; everything was possible.

It is crucial to understand this.

From this state where duality exists — not as a moral division, not as conflict, but as the first differentiation necessary for manifestation. Stillness alone cannot produce form; motion alone cannot sustain order. Creation would begin only when these two tendencies resolve.

CHAPTER 2

THE BIRTH OF DUALITY**

Creation does not begin with form; it begins with difference. From the silent state described earlier, existence could not unfold until a fundamental distinction existed. That distinction is duality—not as opposition, not as conflict, but as the first necessary condition for manifestation.

The state before creation is whole, yet silent. For anything to appear, there must be a state. For anything to appear, there must be differentiation within the state. Duality is that moment of differentiation—the point where stillness gives rise to movement, and movement requires stillness in return.

This duality is not moral. It is not good versus evil, virtue versus vice, or light versus darkness in the ethical sense. Those interpretations arise much later, within human consciousness. At the cosmic level, duality is structural and inevitable. It is the emergence of two complementary tendencies:

One has a tendency toward expansion, expression, dynamism, and desire.

The other tends towards restraint, stability, order, and stillness.

Neither can exist meaningfully without the other. Expansion without restraint would dissolve into chaos; restraint without expansion would freeze into inertia. Creation requires both. Duality is therefore not a flaw in existence but its enabling principle.

Spiritual insight has long recognised this truth. Many traditions speak of complementary forces—active and passive, masculine and feminine, movement and rest. Though symbols differ, the intuition is the same: reality unfolds through paired principles that sustain each other through tension and balance.

Scientific understanding, in its own language, echoes this structure. Energy and matter, action and reaction, expansion and contraction—every fundamental process reveals polarity. Even stability in nature is maintained not by uniformity, but by equilibrium between opposing forces. Science observes the pattern; philosophy seeks its meaning.

It is important to understand that duality did not arise as a rebellion against unity. It emerged within unity. The silent state did not fracture; it differentiated. Just as a single note may give rise to harmony without losing its identity, unity expressed itself as polarity without ceasing to be whole.

This is why duality is eternal. It is not a temporary phase that will be "resolved" someday. As long as creation exists, duality must exist. What changes is not duality itself, but the level at which it is understood. When misunderstood, it appears as conflict; when understood, it appears as balance.

The dynamic principle—the force of movement—introduces change, novelty, and becoming. Without it, there would be no evolution, no creativity, no diversity. But this force alone cannot sustain existence. It must be held, shaped, and guided.

The stabilising principle—the force of restraint—introduces order, continuity, and coherence. Without it, creation would lack form and persistence. But restraint alone cannot create. It preserves; it does not initiate.

Thus, creation is born not from the dominance of one force over the other, but from their interaction. Duality is not a battle; it is a dialogue.

This dialogue is subtle at the cosmic level, yet it sets the pattern for everything that follows. Matter and energy, time and space, life and death, growth and decay—all are later expressions of this primordial duality. Even consciousness, as it evolves, will reflect this structure within itself.

A crucial misunderstanding arises when the human mind seeks to eliminate one side of duality in pursuit of purity or perfection. Such attempts—whether philosophical, religious, or ideological—inevitably fail. To deny one pole is to deny creation itself. Harmony lies not in erasing duality, but in understanding its necessity.

The birth of duality marks the moment when existence becomes expressive. It is the threshold where silence prepares to speak, where stillness prepares to move. From here onward, the universe is no longer unmanifest—it is poised for creation.

In the next movement, this duality will no longer remain abstract. Through interaction, tension, and balance, it will give rise to the first act of manifestation—the emergence of the universe itself.

Creation does not happen despite duality.

Creation happens because of it.

CHAPTER 3

FUSION AND CREATION**

The moment the divine primordial entity resolved that there shall be creation, physical laws came into force. The subsequent fusion of primordial entities executed the resolve, releasing the order of energy beyond human cognition.

The word fusion should not be misunderstood as violence. It does not imply chaos or accident. Rather, it signifies contact—an inevitable interaction between complementary tendencies that cannot remain separate once differentiation has occurred. When movement meets restraint, expression meets structure, and potential meets limitation, manifestation becomes possible.

From a philosophical perspective, creation is not an act imposed from outside, but a natural consequence of interaction within existence itself. Duality contains tension, and tension seeks release through expression. The universe is that expression.

Science offers analogies that, while incomplete, are instructive. Modern cosmology speaks of an initial expansion—a moment when the universe began to unfold from an extremely concentrated state. It describes energy differentiating into matter, forces separating, space expanding, and time becoming measurable. These descriptions do not explain why creation occurred, but they do illustrate how interaction gives rise to structure.

What philosophy adds is meaning. The expansion described by science corresponds to the dynamic principle—the outward movement inherent in duality. The formation of laws, constants, and stable structures corresponds to the restraining principle—the restraining force that gives coherence and continuity. Without both, there would be no universe capable of sustaining itself.

Creation, therefore, is not a single moment frozen in the past. It is an ongoing process. The same interaction that gave birth to the cosmos continues at every level of existence. Stars form and dissolve, galaxies emerge and fade, matter organises and reorganises—all through the continuous interplay of expansion and restraint.

It is tempting to imagine the universe as having begun with disorder that gradually settled into order. But this view is misleading. Order was present from the beginning—not as a rigid structure, but as an inherent balance. Chaos and order are not opposites in creation; they are phases within a larger harmony governed by duality.

The dynamic force pushes existence outward, creating diversity, complexity, and novelty. The stabilising force pulls inward, shaping, limiting, and preserving. Their interaction generates rhythm. Creation is rhythmic, not linear. It pulses, expands, contracts, evolves, and reorganises. This rhythm is visible everywhere—from cosmic cycles to biological life.

An important consequence follows: since creation arises from interaction, no created form is absolute. Everything that emerges is provisional—subject to change, transformation, and eventual dissolution. Permanence belongs only to the underlying duality and the silent ground from which it arose. Forms come and go; principles endure.

This insight dissolves a deep human anxiety—the fear that creation must be defended against change. In truth, change is not the enemy of existence; it is its expression. What resists change suffers; what understands change participates in creation consciously.

At this stage, the universe is no longer silent, yet it is not chaotic. It is ordered movement, structured dynamism. Matter condenses, energy flows, and the stage is set for complexity to arise. Time begins to make sense because change becomes measurable. Space gains meaning because expansion creates distance and relation.

The fusion of dual forces does not end with the birth of the universe; it sustains it. Every process within creation is a renewed meeting of these tendencies. Where balance is maintained, systems endure. Where imbalance grows, transformation follows.

Thus, creation is not a completed event to be admired from a distance. It is a living process in which existence continuously participates. The universe is not merely created; it is creating.

In understanding creation as interaction rather than origin, the human mind takes a step closer to humility. It recognises that it lives within an unfolding process far greater than any single form or moment. Creation is not behind us; it is happening now.

From this ongoing creation arise the fundamental dimensions that shape all experience—time, space, and law. To these, we now turn.

CHAPTER 4

TIME, SPACE, AND LAW**

With creation underway, existence acquires structure. The interaction of dual forces does not merely produce matter and energy; it gives rise to the fundamental dimensions through which creation becomes intelligible—time, space, and law. These are not causes of creation; they are consequences of it.

Time is often imagined as something that existed before the universe, waiting for events to occur within it. This is a human projection. Time has meaning only where change exists. Before creation, in the silent stage, there was no sequence, no before or after. Stillness does not age. Time was born when movement began to be measured against continuity.

The dynamic principle introduces change; the stabilising principle provides reference. Time arises from their relationship. Without change, there is no time; without continuity, change cannot be recognised. Thus, time is not an independent entity but a measure of transformation within order.

Space emerges similarly. It is not an empty container in which creation unfolds. Space is the expression of expansion. As the dynamic tendency moves outward, distance appears. As the stabilising tendency holds form, relations become possible. Space is therefore relational, not absolute. It exists because things exist in relation to one another.

Scientific observation confirms this insight indirectly. Space expands with the universe; it bends with matter; it is inseparable from energy. These discoveries hint at a deeper truth: space is not separate from creation—it is one of its modes of expression.

Law arises from the need for balance. Where dual forces interact, patterns emerge. These patterns, when stable, are perceived as laws. Natural laws are not imposed from outside; they are the consistent expressions of equilibrium between opposing tendencies. Gravity, conservation, symmetry, and causality all reflect balance maintained through tension.

It is crucial to understand that laws are not rigid commands but living regularities. They endure as long as the underlying balance endures. When conditions change beyond a threshold, new laws appear—not because order collapses, but because balance reorganises at a different level.

This explains why creation is intelligible. The universe is not random; it is an ordered movement. Yet it is not static; it is evolving order. Law exists not to freeze existence, but to make change coherent.

Time gives creation direction without destiny. Space gives creation form without confinement. Law gives creation order without rigidity. Together, they make experience possible.

A subtle implication follows. Because time, space, and law arise from duality, they are not eternal in their present form. They belong to the realm of manifestation. When creation dissolves, they dissolve with it. What remains is not time or space, but the silent ground and the principles that gave rise to manifestation.

This insight has profound philosophical consequences. It means that the ultimate reality is not bound by time. It means that existence is not confined to spatial form. And it means that law, however precise, is not absolute—it is contextual.

Understanding time, space, and law as emergent rather than fundamental frees the mind from a deep illusion—the illusion that existence is a mechanical system running independently of meaning. In truth, structure arises to serve expression, and expression arises from a deeper order.

With this structure in place, creation enters rhythm. Expansion and restraint now operate within time, across space, and through law. This rhythm produces cycles of formation and dissolution, growth and decay, emergence and return.

It is to these cycles, which reveal the continuity of creation beyond individual forms, that we now turn.

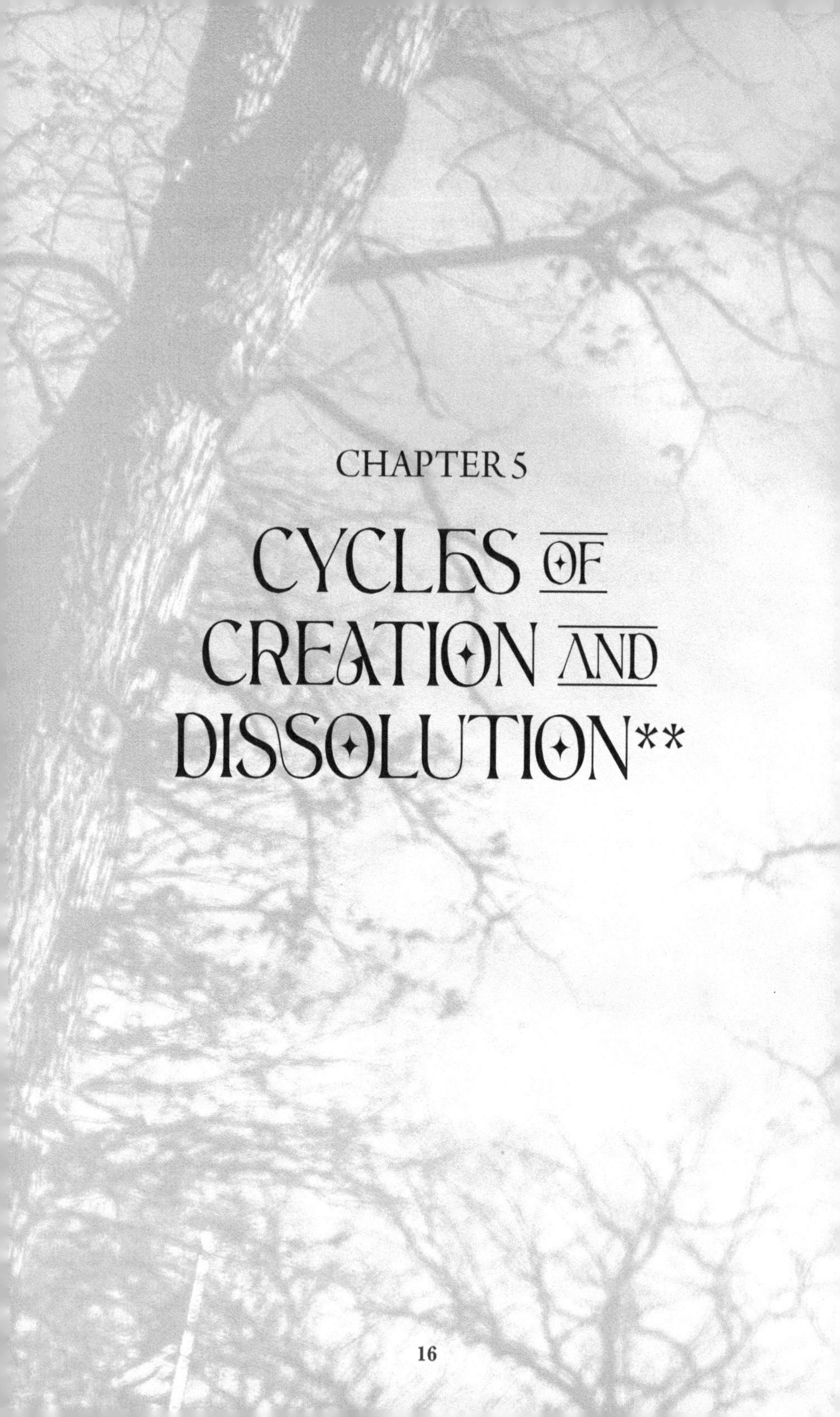

CHAPTER 5

CYCLES OF CREATION AND DISSOLUTION**

Creation, once understood as interaction rather than a single event, reveals its deeper nature: it is cyclical. The universe is not a straight line moving from beginning to end; it is a rhythm of emergence, stability, decline, and renewal. Cycles are not accidents of creation—they are its method.

Every form that arises does so under the influence of dual forces. The dynamic principle drives expansion, growth, and complexity. The stabilising principle consolidates, preserves, and maintains order. But neither force remains dominant indefinitely. Expansion reaches a limit; stability hardens into rigidity. When balance is lost, dissolution begins—not as punishment, but as correction.

Dissolution is often misunderstood as destruction. In truth, nothing essential is destroyed. What dissolves is form, not essence; structure, not principle. Dissolution is the return of manifested complexity to a simpler state from which new creation can arise. It is not the negation of existence, but its renewal.

Nature provides countless illustrations. Stars are born, burn, collapse, and scatter their elements, which later form new stars and planets. Biological life grows, matures, decays, and feeds new life. Civilisations rise, flourish, fragment, and fade—only to leave behind ideas, values, and lessons that shape future cultures. Everywhere, the same pattern repeats.

This rhythm exists because permanence at the level of form would freeze evolution. If creation never dissolved, learning would cease. If structures never broke down, stagnation would prevail. Change is not an enemy of order; it is its partner.

From a philosophical standpoint, cycles arise because duality itself is dynamic. Expansion seeks expression, but expression eventually exhausts its potential. Restraint seeks stability, but stability eventually becomes confinement. Dissolution restores balance by releasing what has become rigid and clearing the ground for new expression.

This understanding corrects a deep human fear: the fear of endings. Endings are not failures of creation; they are integral to it. What ends at one level continues at another. Nothing is absolutely created; nothing is absolutely destroyed. Existence transforms.

Time makes cycles visible, but cycles are not created by time. Time is the measure of transformation; cycles are the pattern of transformation. When time dissolves at the end of a cosmic phase, the principles that governed creation remain intact, ready to express themselves again.

The silent ground from which creation emerged is never lost. It remains present beneath every cycle, unchanged by the rise and fall of forms. Duality, too, remains constant. What changes is the configuration of manifestation—the particular expression of balance at a given moment.

This insight has a liberating consequence for human understanding. It means that collapse is not meaningless, decline is not final, and loss is not absolute. Wherever imbalance reaches its extreme, renewal becomes possible. Crisis is not the end of order; it is the signal that order must reorganise at a deeper level.

The universe does not move toward perfection in a straight ascent. It evolves through learning. Each cycle refines awareness by exposing the limits of previous forms. What cannot adapt dissolves; what can adapt transforms.

At the cosmic level, these cycles may span unimaginable durations. At the human level, they are compressed into lifetimes, societies, and histories. Yet the pattern remains the same. What is born must mature; what matures must eventually release its form.

Understanding cyclic creation dissolves the illusion of finality. There is no ultimate collapse beyond which nothing exists. There is no final creation after which nothing new can arise. Existence moves, rests, renews, and moves again.

With this understanding, the mind begins to see continuity beneath change. It recognises that behind all forms stands a process greater than form—a process governed by duality, sustained by balance, and renewed through cycles.

This recognition prepares the ground for a deeper inquiry. If forms dissolve but something continues, what is it that endures? What carries learning across cycles? What bridges creation and dissolution?

To answer these questions, we must turn our attention from form to consciousness—the thread that runs through all transformation.

CHAPTER 6

CONSCIOUSNESS BEYOND MATTER**

With the recognition that all forms arise and dissolve in cycles, a fundamental question emerges: what, if anything, continues through these transformations? Matter changes, energy transforms, structures collapse and re-form. Yet the universe does not merely repeat; it learns, refines, and deepens. That continuity points toward something more subtle than form—consciousness.

Consciousness is often treated as a by-product of matter, an accidental outcome of biological complexity. This view, while convenient, is incomplete. It explains correlation but not origin. It describes how consciousness appears in organised systems, but not why awareness exists at all. If matter alone were sufficient, awareness would be redundant. Yet awareness is irreducible; it cannot be eliminated without eliminating experience itself.

Consciousness is the primary and universal reality, and awareness is its expression as matter. In humans, this awareness differentiates into physical and spiritual consciousness, and in all other matter, it remains indivisible.

This does not mean consciousness is a separate substance floating above the universe. It is not an external observer. It is woven into existence as its inner dimension. Just as the source arises from expansion, following divine fusion, experience arises from consciousness. One without the other yields an incomplete picture of reality.

Scientific analogies again offer partial insight. Physics describes fields that permeate space, invisible yet fundamental. Consciousness may be understood in a similar way—not as a measurable field, but as a pervasive condition that allows experience to occur wherever organisation reaches sufficient sensitivity. The analogy is imperfect, but it points in the right direction: consciousness is expressed through individual forms.

This perspective explains continuity across cycles. When forms dissolve, consciousness does not vanish; it withdraws from expression. When new forms arise, consciousness re-enters expression, shaped by accumulated conditions. What persists is not memory in the human sense, but potential refined by experience. Learning is conserved, even when form is not.

From this view, evolution acquires a deeper meaning. It is not merely the survival of structures, but the refinement of awareness through structure. Complexity increases not for its own sake, but to allow richer modes of experience, perception, and understanding.

This also clarifies why suffering and conflict appear inseparable in growth

Importantly, consciousness beyond matter is not personal in its essence. Personality belongs to form; awareness belongs to being. Individual consciousness is a localised expression, shaped by biological, psychological, and cultural conditions. Beneath these variations lies a continuity that is not owned by any single form.

This understanding dissolves the fear that consciousness begins and ends with the body. What begins is expression; what ends is configuration. Awareness itself is not born in time, nor does it perish in time. It participates in time, but is not contained by it.

Such a view does not negate science; it completes it. Science describes the outer mechanics of existence with increasing precision. Philosophy and spirituality address the inner dimension that science, by its method, must leave aside. Together, they offer a fuller vision of reality—one in which matter and consciousness are not rivals, but partners.

Recognising consciousness as continuous also reshapes ethics. Actions are no longer isolated events with local consequences. They become contributions to an ongoing process of awareness. What is done in ignorance perpetuates ignorance; what is done in understanding refines understanding. Responsibility is no longer imposed from outside; it arises naturally from insight into continuity.

With consciousness acknowledged as enduring, a new question arises: how does this continuity express itself as values, choices, and moral distinctions? Why do human beings experience inner conflict between constructive and destructive tendencies?

To answer this, we must examine how cosmic duality reappears within consciousness itself—first as good and bad, not as absolutes, but as inseparable forces in the evolution of awareness.

CHAPTER 7

GOOD AND BAD: AN INSEPARABLE PAIR**

With consciousness understood as continuous and before form, the question of **good and bad** must be revisited at its roots. In human life, these appear as moral categories, often treated as absolutes locked in opposition. Yet this view, though emotionally compelling, obscures their deeper nature. Good and bad are not enemies in a cosmic struggle; they are **inseparable expressions of duality within consciousness**.

At the level of creation, duality appears as movement and restraint. At the level of consciousness, the same duality appears as constructive and destructive tendencies, integration and fragmentation, clarity and confusion. What humans call "good" and "bad" are experiential interpretations of these tendencies as they operate within awareness.

Good represents movement toward harmony, coherence, and understanding. Bad represents movement toward imbalance, excess, and fragmentation. Neither arises independently. Without the possibility of imbalance, harmony would be meaningless. Without error, understanding could not deepen. As stated in our previous work, a divine spark exists in every living creature. In humans, this spark is present in a dormant form, but it can be awakened to its fullest glow. Through individual effort. Consciousness is present in all, yet its active expression varies as individuals differ in ingenuity, description and capacity for realisation.

This is why moral duality cannot be reduced to simple judgment. To label bad as something that should never exist is to deny the process of learning itself. Error is not the opposite of truth; it is one of its teachers. Conflict is not the negation of growth; it is often its catalyst.

Yet this insight must be handled carefully. To recognise the necessity of bad is not to justify cruelty or indifference. There is a profound difference between **understanding necessity** and **excusing harm**. Consciousness evolves by recognizing destructive tendencies, not by glorifying them. Awareness does not abolish responsibility; it deepens it.

In human experience, good and bad are felt as inner tension. Desire pulls outward, seeking fulfilment, possession, recognition. Restraint pulls inward, seeking balance, moderation, and coherence. When desire overwhelms restraint, actions become harmful. When restraint overwhelms desire, life becomes rigid and lifeless. Moral maturity lies not in eliminating either force, but in **bringing them into conscious balance**.

This explains why ethical systems based solely on commandments often fail. They attempt to suppress one side of duality rather than understand it. Suppression breeds hypocrisy; denial strengthens what it tries to erase. Genuine morality arises not from fear of punishment, but from insight into consequence.

When consciousness is not fully understood, bad appears attractive because it promises immediate gratification. When consciousness is realised, the same actions lose their appeal because their cost becomes visible. Thus, moral evolution is not imposed from outside; it unfolds from within awareness itself.

At the collective level, societies mirror this process. Periods of excess, aggression, or exploitation are followed by collapse, reflection, and reform. History is not a straight march toward virtue; it is a series of corrections. Civilizations learn as individuals do—through imbalance and recovery. As stated in our previous work, a divine spark exists in every living creature in humans this spark is present in a dormant form but it can be awakened to its fullest glow. Through individual effort. Consciousness is present in all yet its active expression whereas individual differ in , description and capacity for realization.

A critical misunderstanding arises when humans seek to create a world entirely free of bad. Such attempts inevitably lead to coercion, dogma, and violence, because they deny a fundamental truth: duality cannot be eliminated without eliminating life itself. What can be transformed is not duality, but the **degree of consciousness with which it is lived**.

Good and bad, therefore, are not fixed categories. They are dynamic orientations within awareness. What is constructive at one stage may become destructive at another. What once appeared necessary may later appear excessive. Wisdom lies in perception, not in rigid judgment.

This understanding brings humility to moral discourse. It dissolves the illusion of moral superiority and replaces it with responsibility. When one recognizes that the same forces operate within oneself, condemnation gives way to comprehension, and comprehension opens the door to change.

Ultimately, good and bad are instruments through which consciousness refines itself. They are not final destinations, but phases in an ongoing journey. As awareness deepens, the pull of destructive tendencies weakens—not because they are forbidden, but because they are understood.

From this point onward, the inquiry naturally turns toward evolution—not merely of forms or species, but of **consciousness itself**. How does awareness grow through experience, error, correction, and insight?

That question leads us to the next stage of understanding.

CHAPTER 8

EVOLUTION AS REALISATION OF CONSCIOUSNESS**

Evolution is commonly understood as the gradual development of forms of matter organising into life, of life diversifying into species, of organisms adapting to environments. This understanding is accurate, but incomplete. It describes the *outer* movement of evolution, not its *inner* direction. Beneath the evolution of form lies a more subtle and decisive process: the **realisation of consciousness**.

Forms evolve because consciousness seeks clearer modes of expression. Each form provides a particular lens through which awareness can experience, respond, and learn. When a form becomes inadequate for further refinement, it is altered or abandoned. Thus, evolution is not driven by chance alone, nor by blind necessity, but by an underlying movement toward greater clarity, sensitivity, and integration.

This does not imply a predetermined goal or final perfection. Consciousness does not evolve toward an endpoint; it evolves through *understanding*. Understanding is never complete, because existence itself is inexhaustible. Evolution, therefore, is not a ladder with a final rung, but a spiral in which insight deepens through repeated engagement with duality.

At early stages, consciousness is almost entirely embedded in form. Reaction dominates perception. Experience is immediate and unreflected. As forms grow more complex, consciousness gains distance from impulse. Memory develops, anticipation appears, and choice becomes possible. Each increase in complexity allows awareness to see itself more clearly.

Yet complexity alone is not realisation. Intelligence without awareness of consciousness can amplify imbalance. This is evident in human history, where technological and intellectual advances have often outpaced moral understanding. Evolution of consciousness is not guaranteed by progress of form; it requires **integration**—the conscious balancing of opposing tendencies.

Duality remains the engine of this refinement. Constructive and destructive impulses continue to operate, but their expression changes. What was once acted out unconsciously can later be observed, questioned, and redirected. Refinement occurs when awareness learns to recognise its own movements without being enslaved by them.

Error plays a central role in this process. Consciousness does not evolve by avoiding mistakes, but by encountering their consequences. Each imbalance reveals a limit. Each limit invites correction. Learning is conserved not as memory alone, but as transformed orientation. What was once compelling loses its force when its cost is understood.

This is why suffering, though never desirable, is often instructive. It exposes disharmony that pleasure can conceal. Pain draws attention inward, forcing reflection where comfort encourages distraction. From this perspective, suffering is not imposed by a hostile universe; it arises when consciousness collides with the limits of its own understanding.

As realisation deepens, the quality of experience changes. Awareness becomes less reactive and more responsive. Desire loses its compulsive grip and becomes intentional. Restraint ceases to feel like denial and becomes discernment. Freedom is no longer confused with indulgence; it is recognised as clarity of choice.

At the human level, this realisation manifests as moral sensitivity, empathy, and responsibility. These are not social inventions imposed from outside; they are expressions of consciousness perceiving its continuity with others. When awareness recognises itself in different forms, exploitation becomes incoherent, and cruelty becomes self-contradictory.

Importantly, realisation does not eliminate individuality. It purifies it. Individual perspective remains, but it is no longer isolated. The self is experienced not as a fortress to be defended, but as a point of participation in a larger process. Identity becomes flexible without becoming diffuse.

Evolution, understood in this way, is not a competition between forms, but a conversation within consciousness. Each form contributes a particular experience; none possesses the whole. Progress lies not in dominance, but in mutual enrichment.

This understanding also clarifies why periods of apparent regression occur. While consciousness itself remains unchanged, expression through individual is enforced unevenly, marked by oscillation, experimentation, overshoot and correction. While consciousness itself remains unchanged, its expression through individuals unfolds unevenly, marked by oscillation, experimentation, overshoot and correction. What appears as a decline at one level may be preparation for integration at another. Evolution includes forgetting as well as remembering, collapse as well as construction.

Realisation of consciousness is therefore not smooth or predictable. It is organic. It unfolds through cycles, just as creation does. What matters is not the absence of error, but the capacity to learn from it.

As awareness is realised gradually, a new question emerges—one that touches the deepest human concern. If consciousness continues beyond forms, and if evolution is understood as further realisation of awareness rather than perfection of structure awareness rather than perfects structure, what is the meaning of death? Is it an end, or another transformation within the same process?

To address this, we must turn directly to the question of **death, transformation, and continuity**.

CHAPTER 9

DEATH, TRANSFORMATION, AND CONTINUITY**

Death has always stood at the edge of human understanding—feared, denied, ritualised, or romanticised, yet rarely understood. This is because death is usually approached as an event rather than as a **process**. When seen in isolation, it appears final; when seen within the larger rhythm of existence, it reveals itself as transformation.

From the perspective developed so far, death cannot be the opposite of life. Life itself is a phase within a larger movement. Forms arise, persist for a time, and dissolve. What ends is not existence, but a particular configuration of existence. To mistake the dissolution of form for the annihilation of being is to confuse appearance with essence.

Everywhere in nature, death is already present—not as catastrophe, but as transition. Cells die so organisms may live. Leaves fall so trees may renew themselves. Stars collapse so new elements may be forged. Dissolution is not an interruption of order; it is one of its expressions. Creation and dissolution are not two separate acts—they are alternating phases of the same rhythm.

Human fear of death arises largely from identification with form. The body, the personality, the accumulated memories and roles—these are experienced as the self. When these are threatened, the self feels threatened. Yet earlier inquiry has shown that consciousness is not identical with form. Form is the vehicle; consciousness is the traveller.

What then dies? The body returns to the material processes from which it arose. The personality—shaped by culture, memory, and circumstance—loses its coherence. Individual identity, as a fixed structure, dissolves. But awareness itself does not vanish; it withdraws from that particular configuration.

This withdrawal should not be imagined as movement through space or time. Consciousness does not "go" anywhere in the physical sense. It simply ceases to express itself through a given form. What remains is continuity without localisation—being without structure.

This continuity is not personal in the familiar sense. Personal memory belongs to form. What persists is not biography, but **orientation**—the refinement achieved through experience. Just as a skill learned is not lost when a particular action ends, awareness does not lose what it has understood when a particular life concludes.

From this perspective, death is neither punishment nor reward. It is released. It releases consciousness from a form that has exhausted its capacity for further refinement. When conditions allow, consciousness re-enters expression, shaped—but not imprisoned—by what has been learned.

This view does not require belief in the literal repetition of personal identity. It does not promise the survival of the ego. Instead, it points to continuity of awareness beyond the ego. The self that demands immortality is precisely the self that must dissolve for understanding to deepen.

Such an understanding transforms the meaning of life itself. Life is no longer a desperate attempt to secure permanence. It becomes an opportunity for participation—an interval in which consciousness engages with limitation to know itself more clearly.

Fear diminishes when death is seen as a transition rather than an erasure. Responsibility deepens when actions are understood as contributions to a continuing process. Meaning shifts from accumulation to refinement, from possession to perception.

This also reframes grief. Loss is real at the level of relationship and form, and it must be honoured. But despair arises only when loss is interpreted as absolute. When continuity is understood, grief becomes softer—not absent, but less corrosive. Love, anger and emotions are biological functions of the brain. They are survival – derived expressions of the organism and perish with its dissolution.

Importantly, this understanding does not diminish the value of life. On the contrary, it heightens it. Because forms are temporary, attention becomes precious. Because expression is finite, presence becomes sacred. Death gives weight to living without reducing it to fear.

In the larger arc of existence, death is a moment of silence between two expressions—akin to the silent ground before creation. Just as creation arose from stillness, new expression arises from dissolution. The circle is not broken; it is completed.

With this recognition, the inquiry reaches a turning point. Having traced duality from cosmic creation through consciousness, morality, evolution, and death, the focus must now shift decisively inward—to the **human being**, where all these forces converge consciously.

The universe has become aware of itself in the human mind. How this awareness is handled—confused or clarified, divided or integrated—will determine the next phase of evolution.

This chapter revisits ethical and psychological insights long articulated in classical spiritual literature, particularly in Bhagavath Geetha and presents them in a contemporary experiential context. The intent is not to rotate doctoral but to re-examine enduring observations on human conduct, emotion, and attachment in the light of modern light and social realities.

We now turn to the human being as **microcosm**.

CHAPTER 10

THE HUMAN BEING AS MICROCOSM**

Human beings represent one mode through which cosmic duality becomes experientially articulated. There is no basis assume that such an expression is unique to humanity or confined to earth. In an infinite universe, duality may manifest through numerous phenomenal forms and through forms of intelligence far beyond human comprehension.

Because of the duality, the human feels conflicted. The same dual forces that generated creation express themselves through various forms, including human beings. The process toward expansion appears as desire, ambition and creativity. The impulse toward restraint appears as conscience, reflection, moderation, and order. Human life is the arena in which these forces meet consciously.

Unlike other forms of life, the human being can observe this interaction. He can witness his impulses rather than merely act them out. This capacity for self-observation marks a decisive moment in evolution. Consciousness, having passed through countless forms, now turns back upon itself. The universe begins to **know itself through the human mind**.

This does not make humans superior in worth, but unique in responsibility. With awareness comes choice. With choice comes accountability. Instinct no longer dictates action entirely; reflection intervenes. The human being stands at a threshold—capable of aligning with balance or amplifying imbalance.

The human physiology processes are structured by the same dual processes that operate cosmically. Creation appears inwardly as thought arising from silence. Expansion appears as desire seeking expression. Stability appears as identity seeking coherence. Dissolution appears as doubt, disillusionment. Every psychological process echoes a universal pattern.

This explains why human beings experience inner unrest. Consciousness within them is no longer fully embedded in form, yet not fully free from it. The body demands gratification; the mind seeks meaning. Desire urges movement; awareness urges restraint. The resulting tension is not pathological—it is **evolutionary**.

When this tension is misunderstood, it manifests as anxiety, greed, aggression, and confusion. When it is understood, it becomes creativity, ethical sensitivity, and insight. The same forces operate in both cases; only the level of awareness differs.

The ego arises as a functional centre—an organising principle that allows consciousness to navigate form. It is necessary, but not sovereign. Problems arise when the ego mistakes itself for the whole. Then expansion becomes domination, and restraint becomes fear. Balance is lost.

Awareness corrects this distortion by revealing perspective. When the human being sees himself as a participant rather than a possessor, action changes quality. Desire does not disappear, but it becomes intentional. Restraint does not feel oppressive, but protective. Life regains proportion.

At this stage, morality ceases to be external instruction and becomes internal perception. The human being does not ask, "What should I do?" but "What does understanding require?" Ethics emerges not from obedience, but from clarity.

Society, culture, and history are extensions of this inner process. What unfolds collectively is first rehearsed inwardly. A society driven by unchecked desire reflects individuals driven by unchecked desire. A society capable of cooperation reflects individuals capable of inner balance.

Thus, the fate of civilisations is inseparable from the inner condition of their members. No system can compensate for widespread inner disorder. No ideology can replace self-understanding. The human being is the smallest unit of transformation—and the most decisive one.

In the human mind, evolution becomes conscious. The forces that once acted blindly now wait for recognition. Whether this recognition leads to harmony or collapse depends on how awareness is cultivated.

The next question, therefore, is unavoidable: **how do desire and ego shape moral conflict within the human being, and how can this conflict be understood rather than suppressed?**

That inquiry leads directly to the next chapter.

CHAPTER 11

DESIRE, EGO, AND MORAL CONFLICT**

The moral struggle within the human being does not arise from ignorance, but from a misunderstanding of **desire and ego**. These two forces, essential for survival and individuality, become sources of conflict when they are mistaken for the whole of the self. Moral confusion begins with misidentification.

Desire is the inward expression of the cosmic process toward expansion. It seeks experience, fulfilment, growth, and recognition. Without desire, life would stagnate; creativity would vanish; movement would cease. Desire, in itself, is not a problem. It becomes destructive only when it loses its relationship with awareness.

Ego arises as a necessary organising centre. It gives continuity to experience, coherence to identity, and action direction. Without ego, the human being could not function in the world. But ego, like desire, is a tool—not a master. When the ego claims sovereignty, conflict becomes inevitable.

Moral conflict emerges when desire and ego operate without reflection. Desire seeks gratification; ego seeks preservation and enhancement of identity. Together, they can override sensitivity to consequence. Action becomes self-referential. The world is perceived not as shared existence, but as material for personal validation.

Narrowed and obscure thinking is the root cause of moral failure. When awareness contracts, empathy collapses. The human being does not become evil; he becomes **unaware**.

Attempts to resolve moral conflict through suppression usually fail. To repress desire is to drive it underground, where it gains distorted power. To attack the ego directly is to strengthen its defensiveness. Moral rigidity often produces hypocrisy rather than integrity.

Understanding, not suppression, is the transformative force. When desire is observed, its urgency diminishes. When ego is seen as functional rather than absolute, its grip loosens. Awareness does not destroy these forces; it **places them in proportion**.

As awareness deepens, desire changes quality. It becomes selective rather than compulsive. It seeks depth rather than excess. The question shifts from "Can I?" to "What follows?" Consequence enters perception. This is the birth of responsibility.

Similarly, the ego matures when it recognises its limits. It no longer seeks dominance, but orientation. Identity becomes flexible rather than brittle. The self is no longer threatened by difference; it learns from it. Moral strength arises not from certainty, but from clarity.

Inner conflict, then, is not a sign of failure; it is evidence of consciousness awakening. A being without conflict is either unconscious or rigid. Conflict indicates that opposing tendencies are being noticed rather than blindly enacted. Awareness begins in friction.

The task is not to eliminate conflict, but to **hold it consciously**. In that holding, insight arises. Action becomes deliberate rather than reactive. The human being begins to act from understanding rather than impulse.

At the collective level, unresolved desire and ego scale into competition, exploitation, and violence. Societies institutionalise the same conflicts that individuals refuse to examine. Laws multiply where awareness is absent. Control replaces trust. Order is enforced because inner balance is missing.

True moral culture cannot be engineered externally. It grows from individuals who understand their own impulses. When individuals whose actions have a wider influence act with awareness, social harmony follows naturally. When they do not, no system can prevent decay.

This chapter reveals a crucial truth: **moral conflict is not a defect in human nature; it is the point at which evolution becomes conscious**. The question is not whether conflict exists, but whether it is understood.

Understanding transforms struggle into learning. Learning refines awareness. Awareness restores balance between desire and restraint, ego and conscience.

From this point, the inquiry must expand outward again—from the individual to the collective. How do individual minds, shaped by desire and ego, give rise to societies, institutions, and civilisations? And how does collective consciousness, in turn, shape the individual?

That reciprocal relationship forms the subject of the next chapter.

CHAPTER 12

SOCIETY AS COLLECTIVE CONSCIOUSNESS**

Society is not an entity separate from the individuals who compose it. It is the **external expression of their inner states**, a shared field where countless individual minds interact, reinforce, and magnify one another. What appears outwardly as culture, institution, or system is inwardly a pattern of collective consciousness.

Just as the human mind is shaped by the balance or imbalance between desire and restraint, so too is society. When awareness is widespread, social structures tend toward cooperation, justice, and flexibility. When awareness is scarce, structures harden, power concentrates, and control replaces understanding. Society reflects not ideals, but **prevailing inner conditions**.

At its origin, society emerges from necessity. Individuals gather for survival, security, and shared effort. Over time, this practical cooperation develops into norms, traditions, and institutions. These are not inherently oppressive; they are attempts to stabilise collective life. Problems arise when institutions outlive the consciousness that created them.

When awareness declines, institutions continue mechanically. Rules replace insight. Authority replaces responsibility. What was once guidance becomes domination. Society then appears as an external force acting upon individuals, rather than a shared creation sustained by them.

Collective desire expresses itself as ambition for growth, wealth, power, and recognition. Collective ego expresses itself as identity—nation, religion, ideology, class. These identities provide cohesion, but when unexamined, they also generate division. The same ego that defends the individual now defends the group, often with greater intensity.

Conflict between societies mirrors conflict within individuals. Fear of loss, craving for dominance, and resistance to change operate at larger scales. Wars, exploitation, and systemic injustice are not anomalies; they are magnified expressions of unresolved inner conflict.

Yet just as individual conflict signals the possibility of awakening, social crisis signals the possibility of transformation. Periods of instability force reflection. Old structures are questioned. Assumptions are challenged. Consciousness, having been externalised, is compelled to return inward.

A critical misunderstanding arises when reform is sought only through structural change. Laws, policies, and revolutions may alter outer arrangements, but they cannot substitute for inner clarity. Without awareness, new systems reproduce old imbalances under different names. History repeatedly confirms this pattern.

This does not mean social action is meaningless. It means that action divorced from understanding is incomplete. Sustainable reform arises when external change is accompanied by inner awareness. A conscious society is not one without conflict, but one capable of **learning from conflict**.

Education plays a decisive role here. When education cultivates only skill and competition, society becomes efficient but restless. When it cultivates awareness, empathy, and discernment, society becomes resilient. The quality of collective consciousness depends largely on what is encouraged in the young mind.

Media, too, shapes collective awareness. When it amplifies fear, comparison, and outrage, it deepens fragmentation. When it encourages reflection and dialogue, it supports integration. Society listens to itself through its media; what it hears shapes what it becomes.

The most profound change in society does not occur through slogans or enforcement, but through example. Individuals who live with clarity influence others silently. Awareness spreads not by argument, but by presence. A few balanced minds can stabilise an entire community more effectively than elaborate systems imposed from above.

Seen in this light, society is neither enemy nor saviour. It is a mirror. To blame it entirely is to avoid responsibility; to idealise it is to surrender discernment. Society evolves as individuals evolve. There is no other mechanism.

This insight restores agency without illusion. One does not need to change the whole world to contribute to transformation. One needs to understand one's own participation in it. Every act of clarity reduces collective confusion. Every act of unconsciousness amplifies it.

As collective thinking becomes aware of the faults of a particular system, cooperation begins to replace coercion. Diversity becomes richness rather than a threat. Identity loosens without dissolving. Law becomes supportive rather than punitive. Order arises from understanding, not fear.

Yet societies, like individuals, also experience decline. When desire overwhelms restraint, when ego hardens into ideology, when awareness gives way to habit, decay sets in. Understanding this process is essential, for it prepares the ground for renewal.

We must now confront this directly: **how moral decay arises, how it manifests, and how renewal becomes possible**—not through control, but through awareness.

That inquiry leads us to the next chapter.

CHAPTER 13

MORAL DECAY AND RENEWAL**

Moral decay does not announce itself dramatically. It arrives quietly, disguised as convenience, success, and adaptation. Long before values collapse openly, sensitivity dulls. Actions that once provoked inner resistance begin to feel normal. What changes first is not behaviour, but **awareness**.

Decay begins when excess prevails and restraint weakens morbidity, sets in when desire loses direction, and creativity subsides. At the individual level, this appears as justification—small compromises repeated until they no longer feel like compromises. At the collective level, it appears as normalisation of excess, exploitation, and indifference. Society does not fall because people become openly immoral; it falls because they become **morally inattentive**.

Ego plays a central role here. When identity becomes rigid—personal or collective—it resists self-examination. Criticism is experienced as a threat rather than information. Correction is avoided because it destabilises self-image. In such a state, decline continues unchecked, shielded by pride, ideology, or tradition.

History shows this pattern repeatedly. Civilisations decay not when they lack intelligence, but when intelligence detaches from conscience. Sophistication increases while wisdom recedes. Rules multiply while responsibility shrinks. External order is enforced more harshly as inner order dissolves.

Decay is often misunderstood as corruption imposed by external enemies. This misreading prevents renewal. True decay is inward. It is the loss of inner dialogue—the quiet conversation through which individuals and societies correct themselves.

When reflection disappears, repetition takes over. Habit replaces insight.

Yet decay is not final. Just as imbalance triggers dissolution in cosmic cycles, moral decay triggers the conditions for renewal. Collapse, when it comes, is not merely destructive; it exposes falsity. Structures that relied on pretence cannot survive sustained pressure. Crisis strips away illusion.

Renewal begins not with reform, but with **recognition**. The first sign of renewal is discomfort—the refusal to accept decay as normal. This discomfort is often dismissed as pessimism, but it is the seed of conscience reawakening. Sensitivity returns before structure changes.

At the individual level, renewal begins when one stops justifying and starts observing. Responsibility is reclaimed without self-condemnation. Awareness returns to action. Desire is questioned, not suppressed. Ego is seen, not attacked. Integrity re-emerges as coherence between perception and behaviour.

At the collective level, renewal begins with individuals who refuse to participate in unconscious patterns. They may appear insignificant, but their presence alters the field. Renewal does not require majority agreement; it requires **clarity that is contagious**.

Attempts to engineer renewal through force invariably fail. Moral revival imposed from above becomes repression. Genuine renewal spreads from within. It cannot be accelerated beyond readiness, nor prevented once understanding takes root.

Importantly, renewal does not restore the past. It does not idealise earlier forms. Every renewal is also an evolution. Lessons learned through decay are integrated, not erased. The new order carries scars—but also wisdom.

This is why nostalgia is not renewal. Longing for earlier simplicity ignores the learning embedded in complexity. True renewal retains depth while restoring balance. It simplifies without regressing. It refines rather than rejects.

Seen this way, decay and renewal are not opposites. They are phases of the same corrective process. Decay reveals limits; renewal reorients awareness. Together, they advance consciousness.

The question now becomes decisive: **what responsibility does the human being bear in this process?** If consciousness is advanced through awareness, and if renewal depends on clarity, then the future is not predetermined. It depends on how consciously human beings live.

That realisation leads us to the final chapter.

CHAPTER 14

IRRELIGIOUS SOCIETIES AND THE ILLUSION OF FREEDOM**

Irreligious societies arise as a reaction against religious rigidity. Rejecting inherited belief, they emphasise reason, autonomy, and individual freedom. This rejection can be liberating, but it is not inherently awakening. When religion is discarded without cultivating inner awareness, a different imbalance emerges.

In irreligious societies, external authority weakens, but internal discipline does not necessarily grow. Freedom expands faster than understanding. Desire, no longer restrained by belief, seeks legitimacy rather than insight. What was once forbidden is now normalised without examination.

Moral authority in such societies shifts from religion to **law and utility**. Ethics becomes functional: what is legal, efficient, or socially acceptable. Responsibility is reduced to compliance. Conscience weakens because legality replaces perception. What is permitted is assumed to be right.

Irreligious societies excel in organisation, innovation. Systems function efficiently. Technology advances rapidly. Yet beneath this competence lies restlessness. Meaning is replaced by performance. Success becomes identity. Speed replaces reflection.

Without inward orientation, desire multiplies without direction. Consumption substitutes for fulfilment. Stimulation replaces depth. The individual becomes free to choose, but unclear about what is worth choosing. Anxiety grows not from restriction, but from excess.

Restraint is often misunderstood as repression. Discipline is viewed as a limitation. As a result, impulse governs behaviour more than understanding. The self becomes fragmented, pulled by competing desires. Freedom without self-knowledge turns into compulsion.

Collectively, irreligious societies appear tolerant, yet struggle with cohesion. Identity becomes fluid, but community weakens. Individuals coexist without a deep connection. Compassion becomes abstract rather than lived. Loneliness spreads amid abundance.

Unlike rigid religious societies, collapse here is rarely explosive. It is gradual. Meaning erodes silently. Trust diminishes. Relationships become transactional. Institutions continue to function even as inner vitality fades. Decay expresses itself as exhaustion rather than revolt.

Importantly, irreligion is not equivalent to maturity. Absence of belief does not guarantee awareness. A society can abandon religion and remain unconscious governed by appetite, fear, and habit rather than insight.

Yet irreligious societies, too, carry the seed of transformation. Their emphasis on inquiry and freedom can support awakening if redirected inward. When questioning extends beyond systems into self-observation, freedom regains depth. When restraint is rediscovered as intelligence rather than repression, balance returns.

The failure of irreligious societies lies not in rejecting belief, but in neglecting consciousness. Intelligence grows sharper, but wisdom remains undeveloped. Progress accelerates the imbalance instead of correcting it.

Both rigid religious and irreligious societies fail in different ways for the same reason: **they replace inner awareness with external structures**—belief in one case, systems in the other.

Only when consciousness learns to govern itself does society mature.

CHAPTER 15

THE DESTINY OF HUMANITY

The destiny of human consciousness is not written in prophecy or fixed by fate. It is shaped moment by moment by the quality of awareness with which human beings live. Evolution has brought humanity to a point where it can now participate knowingly in its own development. This capacity marks a turning point—one that carries both promise and risk.

Until now, humanity evolved largely through necessity. It was driven by survival, adaptation, and reaction. Forms changed because they had to. Awareness followed experience. In the human being, this order reverses. Awareness can now **precede action**. Humanity can choose its direction instead of being pushed by circumstance.

This shift changes the meaning of destiny. The same dual forces that shaped creation now await conscious integration. Whether they lead to harmony or collapse depends on how they are lived inwardly.

The future of humanity does not lie in domination of nature, of others, or of technology. Domination is the old language of unconscious expansion. It multiplies power but fragments understanding. True advancement lies in **integration**—the capacity to hold complexity without losing balance.

If desire continues without restraint, intelligence will amplify destruction. If restraint hardens without insight, life will stagnate. The destiny of consciousness depends on balance—on the union of clarity and compassion, intelligence and humility.

This balance cannot be legislated. It cannot be manufactured by systems alone. It must be embodied. Each human being becomes a point where evolution either advances consciously or repeats itself blindly. Responsibility is no longer abstract; it is immediate.

The mature expression of consciousness is not withdrawal from the world, but **participation without blindness**. It is action informed by awareness, ambition guided by conscience, and creativity aligned with consequence. Such consciousness does not reject desire; it refines it. It does not abolish the ego; it places it in the service of understanding.

When lived this way, human consciousness becomes a stabilising force in creation. Conflict does not disappear, but it becomes instructive rather than destructive. Difference does not dissolve, but it becomes dialogue rather than division. Complexity increases without chaos.

This vision is not utopian. It does not promise a world without suffering or error. It recognises that duality remains. What changes is the relationship to duality. Consciousness no longer fights it blindly; it learns from it deliberately.

The destiny of humanity is therefore not to achieve perfection, but **lucidity**. Not immortality of form, but continuity of understanding. Not absolute peace, but intelligent balance.

In this state, humanity no longer sees itself as separate from the universe. It recognises itself as one of the universe's ways of becoming aware. Responsibility expands naturally. Life care is no longer a moral obligation; it is self-recognition.

The human mind, when clarified, becomes a bridge between silence and expression, stillness and movement, creation and return. In such minds, the ancient division between science and spirituality dissolves. Knowledge regains reverence; faith regains intelligence.

This destiny will not arrive dramatically. It will emerge quietly, through countless individual awakenings. It will not be announced by power, but recognised by coherence. Where understanding deepens, the future takes shape.

The circle now closes—not by ending, but by returning to the beginning. Just as creation emerged from silence, conscious living returns the human being to silence—not as withdrawal, but as depth. From that depth, action becomes meaningful.

The duality of existence does not ask to be solved. It asks to be **understood**. In that understanding, consciousness fulfils its role—not as ruler of creation, but as its witness and participant.

This is not the end of the journey.

It is the point at which the journey becomes conscious.